501 Reasons Why
Fathers
Know Best

501 Reasons Why Fathers Know Best

EDITED BY
Ellen Kent and Beth Stephens

BARNES
&NOBLE
BOOKS
NEW YORK

Thanks to Mike Fielo,
a man with a truly junky mind.
E.K.

2003 Barnes & Noble Books

ISBN 0-7607-3607-3

Text design by Rhea Braunstein

Printed and bound in the United States of America

03 04 05 06 07 08 09 MP 9 8 7 6 5 4 3 2 1

BVG

Contents

Contents

Contents

Contents

501 Reasons Why Fathers Know Best

Father Knows Best

Dad makes the best scrambled eggs.

⑥   ⑥   ⑥

He can put you on his shoulders so
you can see over a crowd.

Dad can teach you how to throw
a curveball.

ⓖ   ⓖ   ⓖ

He knows how to give the best
bear hugs.

ⓖ   ⓖ   ⓖ

Dad can fix everything from a broken
toy to a squeaky door.

Dad always manages to know how to scare off prospective dates.

6   6   6

He knows when to hand over the car keys.

6   6   6

And when NOT to hand over the car keys.

Only a dad knows how to give
horseback rides.

⊚　　　⊚　　　⊚

Dad will always help you with your
science projects.

⊚　　　⊚　　　⊚

He can make the best book cover out
of a brown paper bag.

Dad knows the many things that
can be done with a hammer and a
hand drill.

⑥   ⑥   ⑥

He tells the best ghost stories while
camping.

⑥   ⑥   ⑥

He knows how to scare monsters out
from underneath the bed.

Dad is convinced that you're the
prettiest girl in the class.

⑥　　⑥　　⑥

And the best forward on the
soccer team.

⑥　　⑥　　⑥

He can help you pick out a Mother's
Day gift.

He knows how to talk Mom into
letting you get the Super Blaster
Soaker 2000 water gun.

⑥   ⑥   ⑥

Dads know the best way to get the
Frisbee out of the tree.

⑥   ⑥   ⑥

He knows the most painless way to
remove a splinter from your toe.

Dad, a.k.a. . . .

Papa

Pops

Dada

Old Man

Bug-Killer

Official Barbecue-er

The King

Money Tree

Leaky-Faucet Fixer

Lawn-Care Specialist

Master Turkey Carver

Bike-Riding Instructor

A Father Is . . .

A father is a man who expects his son to be as good a man as he meant to be.

Author unknown

⑥　　⑥　　⑥

One father is more than a hundred schoolmasters.

George Herbert, English poet

A father is a guy who has snapshots in his wallet where his money used to be.

Author unknown

ଳ   ଳ   ଳ

That is the thankless position of the father in the family; the provider for all and the enemy of all.

J. August Strindberg, Swedish dramatist

ଳ   ଳ   ଳ

Today, while the titular head of the family may still be the father, everyone knows that he is little more than chairman, at most, of the entertainment committee.

Ashley Montagu, American anthropologist and social biologist

⑥   ⑥   ⑥

The father is the most powerful incarnation of the archetypal masculine.

Carl Jung, Swiss psychiatrist

⑥   ⑥   ⑥

Whether he knows it or not, and no matter what his position in society, the father is the initiating priest through whom the young being passes into the larger world.

Joseph Campbell, American writer,
editor, and teacher

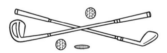

A good father is a little bit of a mother.

Lee Salk, American pediatrician
and family expert

No father should be allowed to get away with the cowardly logic which concludes that his only job in the family is to pay for the bacon. . . . His role is much more grandiose than that. If it is to be properly fulfilled, he should be, in his realm, a man of many faces—an artist, a philosopher, a statesman and, above all, a prolific dispenser of good sense and justice.

Adlai E. Stevenson, American statesman

⑥　⑥　⑥

Fathers are biological necessities, but social accidents.

Margaret Mead,
American anthropologist and writer

Your father is a meat distributor: Well, if you're any indication, he certainly knows his business.

Groucho Marx, American comedian

Things Important to Dad

His golf handicap

ෆ   ෆ   ෆ

The remote control

His daughter's curfew

⟲   ⟲   ⟲

A good parking space

⟲   ⟲   ⟲

Shutting off the lights and turning
down the heat to save money

His son's batting average

⑥ ⑥ ⑥

Warming up the car before driving it

⑥ ⑥ ⑥

Putting the cap on the toothpaste

Teaching his kids how to ride a
two-wheeler

⑥ ⑥ ⑥

Locked doors

⑥ ⑥ ⑥

The sports page

The condition of his son's ear
(i.e., earring-less)

6   6   6

His shirt collars

6   6   6

His old baseball glove and college
football jersey

His kid's grades

⑥   ⑥   ⑥

A clean car

⑥   ⑥   ⑥

The length of his daughter's skirt

Whether or not the Vikings are
trading their best quarterback

6   6   6

His weekly poker game

6   6   6

Control over the barbecue grill

His four-year-old's tee-ball game

⑥   ⑥   ⑥

Electronic gadgets

⑥   ⑥   ⑥

His front lawn

The trash going out, dishes being
washed, and room being cleaned in a
timely manner

🌀 🌀 🌀

His daughter's date arriving on time
and with a firm handshake

Fathers in Song

"Daddy's Little Girl" by Frank Fontaine

"Papa Don't Preach" by Madonna

"Papa, Can You Hear Me?" by Barbra Streisand

"Father's Got His Glasses On" by Cab Calloway

"Oh! My Pa-Pa" by Eddie Fisher

"Papa's Got a Brand New Bag" by James Brown

"Song for My Father" by Horace Silver

"My Heart Belongs to Daddy" by Cole Porter

"A Song for My Daughter" by Ray Allaire

"Papa Loves Mambo" by Perry Como

"Papa Was a Rolling Stone" by the Temptations

Father's Day

Father's Day by the numbers: Ten million ties are purchased, and approximately 119 million phone calls are made each holiday. In 1998, consumers spent an estimated $436.5 million at restaurants in honor of their dads.

Sonora Smart Dodd from Spokane, Washington, is credited with the idea of Father's Day. As she became an adult, she realized the strength and selflessness her father exhibited while raising her and her five siblings, and she wanted to find a way to honor him.

Father's Day is the fifth most popular card-sending holiday, with an estimated $95 million in sales of cards to fathers, husbands, grandfathers, uncles, sons, and sons-in-law.

The first Father's Day was celebrated on June 19, 1910. In 1966, President Lyndon Johnson declared the third Sunday of June as Father's Day with a presidential proclamation.

In a recent survey, when asked what they would most like to receive as a Father's Day gift, 35 percent of dads chose a computer, with a stereo coming in a close second at 27 percent.

Wearing flowers is a traditional way of celebrating Father's Day. Wearing a red rose honors a father still living, while a white flower honors a deceased dad. A white lilac is the official Father's Day flower.

Daddy's Little Girl

Many a man wishes he were strong enough to tear a telephone book in half—especially if he has a teenage daughter.

Guy Lombardo,
American musician and bandleader

⑥ ⑥ ⑥

Daddy (yes, that's what I called him into my adulthood) gave me unconditional love. We had one of those special father-daughter relationships that I believe helped make me the woman and mother I am today.

Carole Simpson, American broadcast journalist

6   6   6

Daughters, I think, are always easier for fathers. I don't know why.

William Plummer, American journalist

6   6   6

It is admirable for a man to take his son fishing, but there is a special place in heaven for the father who takes his daughter shopping.

Author unknown

I can be president of the United States or I can control Alice. I cannot possibly do both.

Theodore Roosevelt,
26th president of the United States

ⓖ　　ⓖ　　ⓖ

It no longer bothers me that I may be constantly searching for father figures; by this time, I have found several and dearly enjoyed knowing them all.

Alice Walker, American author

Perhaps every father should be issued a football mouthguard when his daughter is born, since he's liable to spend the next few decades biting his tongue.

Joe Kelly, author of Dads and Daughters

Old as she was, she still missed her daddy sometimes.

Gloria Naylor, American author

Fathers are key in their children's lives—we know this already. But fathers have a unique influence (for the bad or the good) in a girl's life. A dad is in a powerful position to help his daughter resist the media and cultural pressure to worry exclusively about appearance and sex.

Joe Kelly, author of Dads and Daughters

It's All in the Family—
Political and Historical Relations

Presidents George H. W. Bush and
George W. Bush

Presidents John Adams and John
Quincy Adams

Joseph Kennedy and John F. Kennedy
and John F. Kennedy Jr.

Oliver Wendell Holmes Sr. and Oliver Wendell Holmes Jr.

Al Gore Sr. and Al Gore Jr.

Papa Doc Duvalier and Baby Duvalier

General Benjamin O. Davis (first African-American United States Army general) and General Benjamin O. Davis Jr. (first African-American United States Air Force general)

Jawaharlal Nehru and Indira Gandhi

Sigmund Freud and Anna Freud

General Arthur MacArthur and
General Douglas MacArthur

Things Dad Chooses to Ignore (A.K.A. Dad's Selective Hearing)

Kids fighting in the backseat

ⓖ   ⓖ   ⓖ

Driving directions

ⓖ   ⓖ   ⓖ

Pleas to increase allowance

⟳   ⟳   ⟳

Requests to mow the lawn

⟳   ⟳   ⟳

Talk about women's "personal"
products

A baby crying during the night

6   *6*   *6*

Requests for new clothes

6   *6*   *6*

Complaints about a cold house

Excuses from his kids for why they're
home late or the chores aren't done

⑥　　⑥　　⑥

Any statement including the words
"all my friends have one/are doing
it/are going"

Fun Facts About Dads

According to the *Dallas Morning News*, the number of dads present at their children's births has risen from 27 percent in 1974 to nearly 90 percent today.

Matt Groening named Homer Simpson after his father, Homer Groening, a filmmaker.

Participants of a survey were asked which TV dad best represented the ideal father figure. Cliff Huxtable from *The Cosby Show* came in first with 39 percent. Next was Howard Cunningham from *Happy Days* with 17 percent, and Ward Cleaver from *Leave It To Beaver* followed with 15 percent.

The famous caricaturist Al Hirschfeld hid his daughter's name, Nina, in almost every drawing he did since her birth in 1945.

Werner Hoeger and his 17-year-old son, Chris Hoeger, both competed in the luge in the 2002 Winter Olympics, becoming the first father-and-son team to perform this feat.

A new poll says American dads are having more influence with their children. But a Gallup poll says they haven't caught up to moms yet. While 40 percent of men age 18 to 49 believe their fathers were more influential than their mothers, only 23 percent of men age 50 and older feel that way.

Denny Doherty of the Mamas and the Papas has no children.

New dads are not alone, thanks to a few fathers in Irvine, California. In 1990 they formed Boot Camp for New Dads, workshops where veteran dads show rookie fathers the ropes. Today, Boot Camp is held in more than 160 communities in 36 states.

The word "father" appears more than 2,700 times in Sigmund Freud's complete writings.

Hip-hop star Puff Daddy runs a charity called Daddy's House, which gives money to the kids of New York for computer camps, trips to Africa, and more.

Star Trek: The Next Generation' s star android, Lieutenant Commander Data, wanted a child just as much as his human crew members aboard the Enterprise. He created a daughter, Lal, who became the center of a custody dispute.

Peter Hillary, son of Edmund Hillary (the first man to climb Mount Everest), repeated his father's climb in 1990. The first father and son to summit Mount Everest together were Jean Noel Roche and his son Zebulon in October 1990.

The 2000 Census shows a big increase in the number of single-parent families headed by fathers. Fathers raise their children without a mother in about 2.2 million households, or about one household in 45.

Muddy Waters' big comeback album, which included artists Mike Bloomfield, Paul Butterfield, and Otis Spann, was called "Fathers and Sons."

TV fathers rate well: Robert Young won two Emmy Awards for his role in *Father Knows Best*, and Carroll O'Connor's role as Archie Bunker earned him four Emmy Awards and seven *TV Guide* covers in eight years.

Fathers Around the World

Padre or *Papacita* (Spanish)

Pére (French)

Pai (Portuguese)

Isä (Finnish)

Padre or *Babbo* (Italian)

Baabul (Urdu)

Bapak (Indonesian)

Ojciec (Polish)

Patro (Esperanto)

Tat (Romanian)

Pater (Latin)

Fader (Danish)

Abba (Hebrew)

Athair (Irish Gaelic)

Isa (Estonian)

Vater (German)

Far or *Fader* (Swedish)

Pater or *Vader* (Dutch)

Apa or *Páter* (Hungarian)

Baba (Swahili)

Pa (Afrikaans)

Patera (Greek)

Foter (Yiddish)

Vav (Klingon)

Other Famous "Fathers"

Father Time

Father Christmas

Daddy Longlegs

Daddy Warbucks

Sugar Daddy

Puff Daddy

Fatherland

Father figure

Founding Fathers

Father of the Bride

Father-in-law

Dadaism

Soda Pop

"Pop" sicle

Being a Dad

To become a father is not hard, to be a father is, however.

Wilhelm Busch,
German painter and early cartoonist

🌀   🌀   🌀

. . . Above all, I learned this from my father: Being a dad is the most important job I'll ever have.

George W. Bush,
43rd president of the United States

ⓖ　　　ⓖ　　　ⓖ

A king, realizing his incompetence, can either delegate or abdicate his duties. A father can do neither. If only sons could see the paradox, they would understand the dilemma.

Marlene Dietrich, German-born actor

Being a dad [to son Homer] has made me very sappy and corny. I hope that doesn't seep into the show!

Matt Groening, cartoonist and creator of The Simpsons

I was the same kind of father as I was a harpist—I played by ear.

Harpo Marx, American comedian

Fatherhood is pretending the present you love the most is soap-on-a-rope.

Bill Cosby, American comedian and actor

⑥   ⑥   ⑥

I felt something impossible for me to explain in words. Then when they took her away, it hit me. I got scared all over again and began to feel giddy. Then it came to me—I was a father.

Nat King Cole, American singer and pianist

⑥   ⑥   ⑥

. . . The last three children remaining at home will move out—leaving Mary and I alone to face incessant quiet, able to park the car where we will, listen to the music we want, prepare the exotic meals we dreamed of, talk on the phone once in a while. I'll know where my shirts are; my tools will be in the toolbox when I need them (I guess, in truth, I'm having a hard time finding a dilemma here).

Howard Novel, writer and columnist

ⓖ ⓖ ⓖ

I felt like saying, "I know I don't look great, I don't have a suit and tie on, but I'm this child's father. And you know what? I'm playing on the monkey bars and you're not."

Ad Hudler, author of Househusband

ⓖ　　ⓖ　　ⓖ

My father was frightened of his father, I was frightened of my father and I am damned well going to see to it that my children are frightened of me.

George V, king of Great Britain and Ireland

Fathers should neither be seen nor heard. That is the only proper basis for family life.

Oscar Wilde,
Irish playwright and essayist

The most important thing a father can do for his children is to love their mother.

Reverend Theodore Hesburgh, president
emeritus of Notre Dame University

I have found the best way to give advice to your children is to find out what they want and then advise them to do it.

Harry S. Truman,

33rd president of the United States

To be a successful father . . . there's one absolute rule: when you have a kid, don't look at it for the first two years.

Ernest Hemingway, American novelist and short-story writer

ⓖ　　ⓖ　　ⓖ

The words a father speaks to his children in the privacy of the home are not overheard at the time, but, as in whispering galleries, they will be clearly heard at the end by posterity.

Jean-Paul Richter, German writer and philosopher

You must teach your children that the ground beneath their feet is the ashes of their grandfathers.

Seattle, Native American chief of the Dwamish, Suquamish, and allied Native American tribes

It is a wise father that knows his child.

From The Merchant of Venice
by William Shakespeare

When a father, absent during the day, returns home at six, his children receive only his temperament, not his teaching.

Robert Bly, American poet and translator

ⓖ   ⓖ   ⓖ

So basically you could say that if the job includes the possibility of bodily injury, it's Dad's department. And there's nothing wrong with that, as far as I'm concerned. I like the idea of being the hero.

Sam Harper, columnist and screenwriter

Daddy can't be a family leader or a leader-ship partner with mommy if he allows his focus to drift from what's going on at home. Daddy can't mail in his participation as a parent, either—he has to be actively involved.

Mike Singletary,
former Chicago Bears linebacker

⑥   ⑥   ⑥

Like any father, I have moments when I wonder whether I belong to my children or they belong to me.

Bob Hope, American comedian

If the new American father feels bewildered and even defeated, let him take comfort from the fact that whatever he does in any fathering situation has a fifty percent chance of being right.

Bill Cosby, American comedian and actor

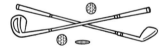

Trying to make it all work, trying to be a senator, trying to be a father, trying to hold those pieces together, I found challenging.

John Kerry, United States senator

Dads are so good at feigning appreciation that they even were able, years ago, to pretend they were happy to receive cologne. This was back in the dark days of cologne-giving, which mercifully came to an end after the horrible 1986 tragedy in Cincinnati wherein a 72-year-old man's house collapsed under the weight of the estimated 2,000 unopened bottles of Old Spice that he had stored in his attic.

Dave Barry,
American humorist and columnist

When you follow in the path of your father,
you learn to walk like him.

Ashanti proverb

I've been a dad for 31 years, five different
times, adopted and non-adopted, four boys
and one girl. I can't imagine what it would be
like without my children.

Angus King, governor of Maine

Dozens of schools offer M.B.A.'s, but there's no Master of Fatherly Administration . . . fathering is tricky work, hellaciously hard sometimes, with more pitfalls and traps than an Indiana Jones flick. We can get training to engineer a merge, turn around a factor, or launch a new brand, but fathering makes all those feats look like cakewalks.

Tom Hirschfeld, American financier

I want [my children] to realize that you don't have to stab anybody in the back to be successful. Just be honest, work hard, and have faith. That will take them further in life than anything.

Denzel Washington, American actor

ⓖ   ⓖ   ⓖ

Funky Smells—Gas vapors, septic tank miasma, crawl space musk, or plain old death in the basement—it's Dad's job to pull that turtleneck collar over his nose and find the source of the offending odor, unless he can convince the dog to do it.

Sam Harper,
American columnist and screenwriter

Their traditional role has changed drastically . . . [father] is happy to sit patiently while his child performs amazing acts of magic for the fifteenth time, or insists that he solve the riddle just learned from the child next door. He regularly attends backyard parties, dining on mud pies decorated with dandelions and sipping imaginary tea from tin cups.

Leo Buscaglia, American writer and educator

@   @   @

I am the comic figure. . . . I think the sort of traditional American father's role of being present to be manipulated by the rest of the family is definitely the role I play.

Calvin Trillin, American journalist

The quality of a child's relationship with his or her father seems to be the most important influence in deciding how that person will react to the world.

John Nicholson,

American architect and children's book author

When children are young, dads regard themselves as giant shock absorbers, there to protect the family from the ruts and bumps on the road of life. But gradually, the role of the father evolves. You begin to see yourself as more like a coach, running your children through practice drills so they'll be better prepared when they have to go out and play the real game. Life's a contact sport, dads will argue, so a few nonfatal bruises along the way merely toughens the body and steels the soul.

W. Bruce Cameron, author of
8 Simple Rules for Dating My
Teenage Daughter

Fathering may be good for men as well as for children.

Author unknown

I have four children and eleven grandchildren. Parenthood is not a matter of balancing but of prioritizing. Fatherhood is job one, and I don't let anything stand in the way.

J. W. Marriott,
founder of Marriott International

Like most dads, I have the opportunity to wear many hats.

Chauffeur.

Doorman for the cats.

Head Dumb Guy when I am asked homework questions such as, "Dad, what is 1.5 divided by .178826?"

Jimmy Patterson, American columnist

Becoming a father made me settle down, go out a lot less and stay out of trouble. My children need a full-time father, and no matter what else I may decide to do or not do, that's one job I'll never take for granted.

Snoop Dogg, American rap artist

⑥   ⑥   ⑥

A Man's children and his garden both reflect the amount of weeding done during the growing season.

Author unknown

When you have a child whose essence is love and generosity, it's a stunning gift. Every scene, everything I do, is influenced by Max.

John C. McGinley, American actor

6   6   6

I consider myself a pretty good parent. I don't beat my kids around the house. My kids haven't turned out like Eddie Munster.

Ozzy Osbourne, rock star

I tell my children every day that I love them. When I kiss them good night or I talk to them on the phone, the last thing we tell each other is how much we love and miss each other.

Kevin Costner, American actor

6   6   6

There is a massive difference between being a father at 24 and at 44. I'm just digging it. I'm more patient.

Mel Gibson, American actor

It was hard. I definitely wouldn't recommend being a young parent. If it does happen, though, I advocate taking full responsibilities for your actions.

Sisqo, American hip-hop artist

ⓖ   ⓖ   ⓖ

I have begun doing all the things I swore always not to do. I carry around baby pictures and show them to people . . . I talk baby talk to Carolina and delight in everything she does . . . she . . . can crawl faster than I can walk. I revel in every new task she learns. . . .

Winston Groom, American novelist

No honor, wealth, lofty title or position at work will ever mean as much to me as "dad."

Stephen R. Covey,

author of The 7 Habits of

Highly Effective People

Favorite TV Dads

Robert Reed as Mike Brady,
The Brady Bunch

Hugh Beaumont as Ward Cleaver,
Leave It to Beaver

Andy Griffith as Sheriff Andy Taylor,
The Andy Griffith Show

Bill Cosby as Cliff Huxtable,
The Cosby Show

Michael Landon as Charles Ingalls,
Little House on the Prairie

John Goodman as Dan Conner,
Roseanne

Fred MacMurray as Steve Douglas,
My Three Sons

Ozzie Nelson as himself, *The Adventures of Ozzie and Harriet*

Homer Simpson, *The Simpsons*

Fred Gwynne as Herman Munster,
The Munsters

Ed O'Neill as Al Bundy, *Married . . .
With Children*

Robert Young as Jim Anderson, *Father
Knows Best*

George Jetson, *The Jetsons*

Carroll O'Connor as Archie Bunker,
All in the Family

James Gandolfini as Tony Soprano,
The Sopranos

Michael Gross as Steven Keaton,
Family Ties

Tim Allen as Tim "The Tool Man"
Taylor, *Home Improvement*

Paul Reiser as Michael Taylor,
My Two Dads

Tom Bosley as Howard Cunningham,
Happy Days

Dick Van Dyke as Rob Petrie, *The Dick
Van Dyke Show*

Ray Romano as Ray Barone,
Everybody Loves Raymond

Bob Saget as Danny Tanner,
Full House

Buddy Epson as Jed Clampett,
The Beverly Hillbillies

Dick Van Patten as Tom Bradford,
Eight Is Enough

Alan Thicke as Dr. Jason Seaver,
Growing Pains

Danny Thomas as Danny Williams,
Make Room for Daddy

Ozzy Osbourne as himself,
The Osbournes

Things Dads Hate

An interrupted football game

ⓖ   ⓖ   ⓖ

Admitting they cannot do everything

ⓖ   ⓖ   ⓖ

Finding "too much" makeup on their daughters

⟲　　⟲　　⟲

Learning firsthand what "full diaper" means

⟲　　⟲　　⟲

Forgetting to buy a Mother's Day card

Unsolicited advice, visits, calls, faxes,
and mail from four grandparents

6   6   6

How long everyone else takes in
the bathroom

6   6   6

Engaging in "meaningful dialogue"

Low-calorie meals

⟲   ⟲   ⟲

Hearing "Mom lets me do it"

⟲   ⟲   ⟲

Discovering that his daughter has
borrowed his razor to shave her legs

Chick flicks

🌀   🌀   🌀

Putting up the Christmas lights

🌀   🌀   🌀

Long answers when a simple "Yes" or
"No" would do

His wife waiting for him to come
home and fix what someone else
could have fixed

⟲   ⟲   ⟲

Shopping

⟲   ⟲   ⟲

Wrapping gifts

Hearing his own curse words coming
from his four-year-old

⑥　　⑥　　⑥

Carting around three muddy soccer
players, a cranky two-year-old, and a
tuba in the backseat of a minivan

⑥　　⑥　　⑥

His daughter's first boyfriend

What Experts Have to Say

A father's job is to prepare, provide and protect. If you don't give that child protection, where else is he or she going to get it from?

Lieutenant Demitri Kornegay,
Maryland police officer

🌀   🌀   🌀

. . . I feel strongly that we should be urging fathers to be equal participants in their baby's care.

Dr. T. Berry Brazelton, American pediatrician and child-development expert

Guys always think that Mom's going to have the corner on instincts. But every guy becomes the expert on his baby.

Chuck Ault, trainer at Boot Camp for New Dads

Prospective fathers, who now can spend hours pondering whether a plastic bathtub is theoretically better for the tot than the kitchen sink, would do well to instead turn their attention to learning "The Wheels on the Bus Go Round and Round."

Sandi Kahn Shelton,
author of You Might as Well Laugh

But no man knows everything, and it is a rite of passage for every child to find that gap in his father's education and drive a truck through it.

Patrick Boyle, editor of Youth Today

When you become a parent, it is your biggest chance to grow again. You have another crack at yourself. Parents are like shuttles on a loom. They join the threads of the past with the threads of the future and leave their own bright patterns as they go.

Fred Rogers, American children's TV host

Fathers are always afraid that they won't know what to do in that early time. But just jump in there, like you were pulling up a carpet or ripping down a wall. Jump in there and learn. The more you do it, the better you'll be at it.

Robert Frank, Ph.D.,
author of Parenting Partners

⟨ʘ⟩   ⟨ʘ⟩   ⟨ʘ⟩

Many dads cheat their daughters by playing differently with them than with their sons. Our daughters deserve rug burns, too; my teenage girl still enjoys trying to push me around, and still wrestles her mom like money rides on the outcome.

Patrick Boyle, editor of Youth Today

Becoming fathers is the most profound, complicated and life-changing time in men's
lives. It is also the least understood (and until
recently, the least researched) topic in the
study of adult development. The journey to
parenthood has more effect upon men's
sense of purpose and meaning in life than
any other transition that they face.

Bruce Linton, Ph.D., founder of the
Fathers' Forum, an online resource

It's important to become friends with your children. You do this by sharing a common interest, treating them as equals, and not taking advantage of your being the older person.

Dr. Robert N. Butler, founding director
of the National Institute on Aging

❧　　❧　　❧

Love and responsibility do not distinguish genders. A father can be as nurturing and caring as a mother.

Cymbeline Villamin, author of
Stay at Home Fathers: A Closer Look

Numerous studies have established beyond a doubt that infants form close attachment bonds with their fathers and that this occurs at the same time that they form attachments to their mothers. Although father and mother usually play different roles in their child's life, "different" does not mean more or less important.

Richard Warshak, author of
The Custody Revolution

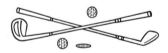

. . . [With the father's involvement] the child is also more likely to have a sense of humor, to develop a sort of inner excitement, to believe in himself or herself, to be more motivated to learn.

Dr. T. Berry Brazelton, American pediatrician and child-development expert

⑥   ⑥   ⑥

I cannot think of any need in childhood as strong as the need for a father's protection.

Sigmund Freud, Austrian physician and founder of psychoanalysis

᧧

Kids spell love T-I-M-E.

Ken Canfield, American author and founder

of the National Center for Fathering

᧤

Favorite Movie Dads

Ralph Richardson as James Tyrone Sr.,
Long Day's Journey into Night

Robin Williams and Billy Crystal as
Dale Putley and Jack Lawrence,
Father's Day

Gregory Peck as Atticus Finch,
To Kill a Mockingbird

Clifton Webb as Frank Bunker
Gilbreth, *Cheaper by the Dozen*

Steve Martin as George Banks,
Father of the Bride

William Powell as Father,
Life with Father

James Earl Jones as Darth Vader,
Star Wars

Dustin Hoffman as Ted Kramer,
Kramer vs. Kramer

Laurence Fishburne as Furious Styles,
Boyz N the Hood

Ryan O'Neal as Moses Pray,
Paper Moon

Samuel L. Jackson as Carl Lee Hailey,
A Time to Kill

Michael Keaton as Jack Butler,
Mr. Mom

Marlon Brando as Vito Corleone,
The Godfather

Adam Sandler as Sonny Koufax,
Big Daddy

Steve Martin as Gil Buckman,
Parenthood

Christopher Plummer as Georg von
Trapp, *The Sound of Music*

Fathers and Sons

If you've never seen a real, fully developed look of disgust, just tell your son how you conducted yourself when you were a boy.

Frank McKinney Hubbard,
American humorist

⑤　　⑤　　⑤

By the time a man realizes that maybe his father was right, he usually has a son who thinks he's wrong.

Charles Wadsworth, American clergyman

For rarely are sons similar to their fathers: most are worse and a few are better than their fathers.

Homer, Greek poet

Fathers send their sons to college either because they went to college, or because they didn't.

Author unknown

6   6   6

His father watched him across the gulf of years and pathos which always must divide a father from his son.

John Marquand, American novelist

6   6   6

Solitary trees, if they grow at all, grow strong; and a boy deprived of a father's care often develops, if he escapes the perils of youth, an independence and vigour of thought which may restore in after life the heavy loss of early days.

Winston Churchill, British statesman

6   6   6

What greater ornament to a son than a father's glory, or to a father than a son's honorable conduct.

Sophocles, Greek dramatist

Every son, at one point or another, defies his father, fights him, departs from him, only to return to him—if he is lucky—closer and more secure than before.

Leonard Bernstein,
American composer and conductor

Perhaps host and guest is really the happiest relation for father and son.

Evelyn Waugh, English novelist

If you love your son, make him leave home.

Japanese proverb

6   6   6

There must always be a struggle between a father and son, while one aims at power and the other at independence.

Samuel Johnson, British lexicographer, critic, and conversationalist

6   6   6

When a father gives to his son, both laugh; when a son gives to his father, both cry.

Yiddish proverb

A bad son and a bad coin will save you some-time or other.

Indian proverb

I cheat my boys every chance I get. I want to make 'em sharp. I trade with the boys and skin 'em and I just beat 'em every time I can.

William A. Rockefeller, American financier

The father who does not
teach his son his duties is
equally guilty with the son
who neglects them.

Confucius, Chinese philosopher

A young boy doesn't come with instructions. He just comes with boundless love and an adventurous spirit. But the journey to manhood begins very early . . . the first time he looks at his dad and thinks, "I want to be like him."
Harry H. Harrison Jr., author of Father to Son

⊚   ⊚   ⊚

Small boys become big men through the influence of big men who care about small boys.

Author unknown

Today, my son already has a lot to complain about because he has me as his father. For one thing, I rarely play baseball with him, as other daddies do. Why? In his own words, "You stink at pitching!" To him, a daddy, or an American daddy, should know how to play this American game. Since I am not good at the game, I may not even be qualified to be a daddy.

Zhu Xiao Di, researcher at Harvard University

⑤   ⑤   ⑤

It is not flesh and blood, but the heart that makes us fathers and sons.

Friedrich von Schiller, German dramatist
and poet

Dad Needs Help

Matching his clothes

🌀   🌀   🌀

Picking out an anniversary gift
for Mom

Understanding the difference
between Barney and the Teletubbies

⊙   ⊙   ⊙

Saying the right thing to his fourteen-
year-old son after his first breakup

⊙   ⊙   ⊙

Working the new DVD player

Choosing wallpaper and curtains for the kitchen

⟲   ⟲   ⟲

Dealing with Grandma (especially Mom's mom)

⟲   ⟲   ⟲

Surfing the Internet

Putting his daughter's hair in pigtails

⑥   ⑥   ⑥

Wrapping Christmas gifts

⑥   ⑥   ⑥

Talking about "the birds and
the bees"

Programming the clock in his car

6   6   6

Dealing with his receding hairline and
increasing waist size

6   6   6

Thinking of something to feed the
kids when Mom's away

It's All in the Family—
Famous Dads and Kids in the Arts

Kirk Douglas and Michael Douglas

Martin Sheen and sons Charlie Sheen and Emilio Estevez

John Astin and sons Sean and Mackenzie Astin

Tony Curtis and Jamie Lee Curtis

Paul McCartney and Stella McCartney

John Huston and Anjelica Huston

Henry Fonda and children Peter and Jane Fonda

John Lennon and Sean Lennon

Sonny Bono and Chastity Bono

John Cheever and Susan Cheever

Richard Simon (founder of Simon & Schuster) and Carly Simon

Vincente Minnelli and Liza Minnelli

Frank Sinatra and Nancy Sinatra

John Phillips and daughters Mackenzie Phillips, Bijou Phillips, and Chynna Phillips

Danny Thomas and Marlo Thomas

Nat King Cole and Natalie Cole

Lloyd Bridges and sons Jeff and Beau
Bridges

Ozzie Nelson and Ricky Nelson

Ryan O'Neal and Tatum O'Neal

Woody Guthrie and Arlo Guthrie

Eddie Fisher and Carrie Fisher

Michael Redgrave and daughters Lynn
and Vanessa Redgrave

N. C. Wyeth and Andrew Wyeth

Pierre Auguste Renoir and Jean Renoir

Bruce Paltrow and Gwyneth Paltrow

Bucky Pizzarelli and John Pizzarelli

Duke Ellington and Mercer Ellington

Aaron Spelling and Tori Spelling

Peter Fonda and Bridget Fonda

Bruce Dern and Laura Dern

Bob Dylan and Jakob Dylan

Jon Voight and Angelina Jolie

John Raitt and Bonnie Raitt

Steven Tyler and Liv Tyler

Brian Wilson and daughters Wendy and Carnie Wilson

Bob Marley and Ziggy Marley

Johnny Cash and Rosanne Cash

Frank Zappa and Dweezil Zappa

Francis Ford Coppola and Sofia Coppola

Fatherly Feats

Father of America: George Washington

Father of Medicine: Hippocrates

Father of History: Herodotus

Father of the Universe: Uranus

Father of Comedy: Aristophanes

Father of Radio: Guglielmo Marconi

Father of Television: Vladimir Zworykin

Father of Computers: Charles Babbage

Father of Manned Space Flight: Robert Gilruth

Father of the Internet: Jon Postel

The Famous on Their Fathers

I didn't know the full facts of life until I was 17. My father never talked about his work.

Martin Freud, son of Sigmund Freud

ⓖ   ⓖ   ⓖ

[My father] was a hard-working, complicated guy who had a lot of conflicting impulses. . . . He was raised as a Mennonite, which is sort of like the Amish, and he spoke German until he went to school. He and I had a contentious relationship.

Matt Groening, American cartoonist and creator of The Simpsons

6   6   6

For some strange reason, at least two biographers have written that my father never came to see me fight until I turned professional, which is totally untrue. My father's loud and dramatic encouragement spurred me on.

Muhammad Ali, American prizefighter

There was never any doubt that my father loved me. He lived through his kids. He didn't do things for himself on the weekend. Instead, he would take us to play tennis, CYO basketball, or baseball. We sensed the joy he got from that. . . . Without a doubt, I know that my dad is the reason that I am where I am today.

John McEnroe, American tennis champion

⑥   ⑥   ⑥

My sister once sent [my father] a telegram from Vassar saying, "Allowance early or bust!" He immediately sent her back a telegram that read, "Bust!"

Katharine Graham, former chairman of
The Washington Post

My father the banker would shudder to see
In the back of his bank a painter to be.

Paul Cézanne, French painter

⊚   ⊚   ⊚

[My father] believed very strongly in his religion and always taught me and my brother and sister to be honorable. He cobbled our shoes and made our leggings. He even made the tombstone for my mother's grave. There wasn't anything he couldn't do.

Peter Rodino, United States congressman

My father was very strong. I don't agree with a lot of the ways he brought me up. I don't agree with a lot of his values, but he did have a lot of integrity, and if he told us not to do something, he didn't do it either.

Madonna, American singer and actor

My father was a statesman, I'm a political woman. My father was a saint. I'm not.

Indira Gandhi, Indian politician and
former prime minister

My father was not a failure. After all, he was
the father of a president of the United States.

Harry S. Truman,
33rd president of the United States

⊙   ⊙   ⊙

We were a real warm Italian family. Dinner
was a real event in our house. It was a time
for all of us to be together and talk about our
day. Pop always got served first. And we
never got up from the table until he got up.

Yogi Berra, American baseball legend

My father and I were always on the most distant terms when I was a boy—a sort of armed neutrality, so to speak.

Mark Twain, American writer and humorist

ⓖ　　ⓖ　　ⓖ

My father always wanted to be the corpse at every funeral, the bride at every wedding and the baby at every christening.

Alice Roosevelt Longworth, daughter of President Theodore Roosevelt

My dad's idea of a good time is to go to Sears and walk around.

Jay Leno, American comedian
and late-night talk-show host

His failure to be reassuring, present even, accessible, approving, companionable, dictated the judgment . . . he became the awesome figure of the no-praise man, creating in me such a need of approval.

Anaïs Nin, American diarist and writer

Watching [my father] work, the great care and pride he took in painting, whether it was a sign or a whiskey bottle or a mural on a tavern wall, made me admire him, though I knew I wouldn't follow in his footsteps.

Muhammad Ali, American prizefighter

6   6   6

My father was great on developing new ideas and new uses for any product. He was very original in his thinking. . . .

R. J. Reynolds Jr., American businessman

I love the fact that when he was home, he was just being Dad. He wasn't performing. I think that because he was so serious with his career, when he was with us, he just wanted to play.

Natalie Cole, American singer and musician

⑥   ⑥   ⑥

His friends see something in my father I have sometimes overlooked: not just a gentle good nature but an integrity that goes down to the bone. Over time, my own perspective has changed. The mildness I'd mistaken for passivity came to look more like quiet self-possession.

Ralph Keyes, American writer

He was a '50s Dad. He worked hard, but didn't spend a lot of time cutting crusts off PBJs. That wasn't his job. And there are moments (during the meltdown hours) when I feel the pull of the '50s and long for that time when Dads only had to make the bacon, not cook it.

Sam Harper, American columnist
and screenwriter

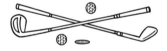

My father seemed nice; he was fun to be around; however, I remember feeling a little bit standoffish. There was something that kept me from buying the whole package. I really did want to like him, but he was a stranger. He was just a man who'd walked into our house with my smile.

Cher, American singer and actor

6   6   6

We'd jump him the minute he came in the mud room, and we'd start wrestling. And he loved to wrestle as much as we did. I think all fathers and sons like to do that.

Roy Rogers Jr., son of Roy Rogers

After the first election, some people said I had ridden into office on Dad's coattails. Perhaps so, but I thought his were the best to be found . . . and I still think so today.

Nancy Kassebaum, United States senator

For as long as I could remember, I harbored a passion for all things related to fashion and style. My father didn't exactly warm to this idea. "I'm not paying for you to go back to undergraduate school to take design courses," he said, "and I don't want to hear about it. You think you're so gifted—go out and get a job."

Vera Wang, American fashion designer

Like all fathers, he has learned to simulate sincere appreciation for gifts that he has absolutely no use for. That's why Dad always responded so positively back when you used to give him—and I hope you no longer do this, although I understand it still happens, even in twenty-first-century America—a tie.

Dave Barry, American humorist and columnist

ⓖ　　ⓖ　　ⓖ

I grew up to have my father's looks—my father's speech patterns—my father's posture—my father's walk—my father's opinions and my mother's contempt for my father.

Jules Feiffer, American writer and cartoonist

My father and I both loved sugar, and sometimes I sneaked sweets from the drawer in my father's dresser where he kept candy hidden among his pairs of socks. The dark chocolate–covered cherries were his favorite, and I often found his cache and depleted it. His socks always smelled of chocolate.

Judy Collins, American composer and singer

My father had an enormous appetite for work. He is probably the only modern President who read every line of the immense national budget—and understood it—before it went up to Congress.

Margaret Truman,
daughter of president Harry S. Truman

6   6   6

There were eight children in the family and my father kept adding on rooms as the family grew. Then as we went off to school he found some rooms on hand and established this hotel.

Conrad Hilton, founder of the Hilton hotel chain

My father, an ambitious and skilled construction equipment operator, raced around the Midwest in his small Ford coupe, working hellishly long hours on road crews, hoping he could save enough in the warm weather months to get through another long winter back home in the small wood-frame hotel his sisters ran for railroad men, traveling salesmen, and local itinerants in the Great Plains village founded by his grandfather. . . .

Tom Brokaw, American broadcast journalist

When I was a kid my father used to say to me, "You'll never amount to anything because you won't stick at anything."

Howard Johnson, founder of the Howard Johnson hotel chain

[My father is] the most charming, funny, incredible guy you'll ever meet.

Tatum O'Neal, American actor

The logical strength of [my father's] mind, the courage of his thought, and the brutal and sometimes repulsive character of his rejoinders impressed me very forcibly. He was far more advanced than I was at his age, and quite out of the common—for good or ill.

Winston Churchill, British statesman

My father was really funny, and I guess it was a competitive thing with him. But a good competitive thing.

Jim Carrey, American comedian and actor

Is it possible for one person to be shy, cautious, moody, short-tempered, autocratic, demanding, confident, friendly, warm and considerate? Is it possible for a single person to evoke the emotions of awe, affection, hate, fear, and respect in the people around him? Sure it is. I have known one such person: my father, Vince Lombardi.

Vince Lombardi Jr., son of Vince Lombardi,
American football coach

But always during my growing-up years and through college and beyond, what I loved and respected about my father is that he always took what I believed and cared about seriously, even when he disagreed very strongly.

Hillary Rodham Clinton, United States senator

⑥   ⑥   ⑥

I was trying so hard to be strong for [my father], but it was very difficult. My biggest challenge was to just be professional and grown up and not be a scared daughter.

Gwyneth Paltrow, American actor

[My father] referred to many animals he ran across—occasionally including a fish he'd caught—as Fred. He got fancy, though, with the name of the only pedigreed dog we ever owned—a lazy, rather dim English bulldog. Although we referred to the dog as Buck, the name on his papers had been Sir Lancelot. My father, not considering that quite grand enough, extended it to Sir Lancelot O'Pujilus.

Calvin Trillin, American journalist

ⓖ   ⓖ   ⓖ

Once my father was dressed in his uniform and I was on the bus with him, I felt so special. My dad would introduce me to his regulars. . . . Dad would sit in the driver's seat, then hoist me up onto his lap. He'd start up the engine, release the brake, and let me steer.

Al Roker, American television weatherman

My father was in textiles and he moved a lot. I just got the habit of roaming. There's nothing I like better, absolutely nothing I like better than jumping in the truck and driving out. Just going.

E. Annie Proulx, American writer

(6)   (6)   (6)

. . . My dad told me, "You should become a lawyer" . . . as a good father, he wanted to spare me that heartache. . . . Of course as a good daughter, I took this as a challenge. I wanted to prove to him that I could do it, I thought he . . . would love me that much more.

Jennifer Aniston, American actor

When I was a child I loved to watch my father shave. I sat on the closed toilet seat and marveled at the sound of the razor gliding over his face, pushing aside the foamy soap like a shovel in the snow. I adored him, this grand figure who slapped lotion on his cheeks every morning, buttoned his clean white shirt and hugged me good-bye.

Marlo Thomas, American actor

ⓖ　　ⓖ　　ⓖ

When I was a child, my father seemed enthusiastic and excitable. As I got older, he seemed stubborn as a mule and tough as the ex-marine he was.

Kenneth Cole, American fashion designer

. . . My father, Marvin Pierce, was the wisest person I ever knew. I adored him. . . . I don't think anyone could hold a candle to him for his wit and wisdom. He laughed constantly and I think that's what people liked so much about him. That smile. That little joke that made everyone feel good about his or her day.

Barbara Bush, former American first lady

During the years my father and I were with the Orioles, we used to head into the locker room together. He'd always say, "I can't wait to get into my work clothes," meaning, of course, his uniform. After he died, I would remember him saying those words every time I suited up for a game.

Cal Ripken Jr., American baseball player

⑥　　⑥　　⑥

My father expected me to do well at everything. He was a big man, a great athlete, and a fine student. . . . That's what I was up against. I was an only son, and I knew he was always watching.

George Steinbrenner,
owner of the New York Yankees

None of you can ever be proud enough of being the child of *such* a Father who has not his equal in this world—so great, so good, so faultless. Try, all of you, to follow in his footsteps and don't be discouraged, for to be really in everything like him none of you, I am sure, will ever be. Try, therefore, to be like him in some points, and you will have acquired a great deal.

Victoria, British monarch, queen of Great Britain and Ireland

When Charles first saw our child Mary, he said all the proper things for a new father. He looked upon the poor little red thing and blurted, "She's more beautiful than the Brooklyn Bridge."

Helen Hayes, American actor

ⓖ   ⓖ   ⓖ

My father used to play with my brother and me in the yard. Mother would come out and say, "You're tearing up the grass." "We're not raising grass," Dad would reply. "We're raising boys."

Harmon Killebrew,
American baseball Hall-of-Famer

My father was more laid back. So people just really don't know Joe Frazier. I am very much a Frazier.

Jacqui Frazier, American boxer and daughter of former heavyweight champion Joe Frazier

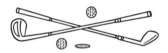

Whenever he would come down the steps, you could always tell. He would have on many jewels or something, and he rattled down the steps.

Lisa Marie Presley, daughter of Elvis Presley

[My father was] even-tempered, optimistic, and even gay.

Anna Freud, psychoanalyst and daughter of
Sigmund Freud

When I was a boy of fourteen, my father was so ignorant I could hardly stand to have the old man around. But when I got to be twenty-one, I was astonished at how much the old man had learned in seven years.

Mark Twain, American writer and humorist

Famous Father One-liners

"Go now, because we're
not stopping."

⑥   ⑥   ⑥

"You call this music?"

"Because I said so, that's why!"

6   6   6

"As long as you're under my roof . . ."

6   6   6

"Don't make me stop this car!"

"Do you think money grows
on trees?"

6   6   6

"Are you trying to heat the entire
world?"

6   6   6

"Do you have any idea how late it is?"

"Shut the door—what do you think
this is, a barn?"

⑥　　⑥　　⑥

"You make a better door than a
window."

⑥　　⑥　　⑥

"Well, if Johnny and Tommy jumped off a bridge, would you?"

⑥   ⑥   ⑥

"Go ask your mother."

⑥   ⑥   ⑥

Father Superlatives

Most Prolific Father: Thought to be Mormon John D. Lee, who had 64 children by 18 wives. Brigham Young is said to have had 57 children, and there is a legend that Moulay Ismail, emperor of Morocco, had 700 sons.

Oldest Father: According to Ripley, the oldest father is said to be mine worker Les Colley from Ararat in Western Victoria, Australia. When his son Oswald was born in 1992, Colley was 93 years old.

Oldest Father of Quadruplets: Toni Del Renzio of England was 70 when his two boys and two girls were born in 1985.

Youngest Father: Thought to be Sean Stewart of Sharnbrook, England, who was 12 when his son was born. Sean was given the day off from school to be at his son's birth.

Youngest Father of Quadruplets: The father of the Belcher quads was 18 when they were born.

Father Never to Talk Back To: Vito Corleone

Most Analytical Father: Sigmund Freud

Tallest Father: Shaquille O'Neal

Most Frightening Father: Darth Vader

Most Intelligent Father: Albert Einstein

Most Motherly Father: Iphagenia Doubtfire

It's All in the Family—
Famous Dads and Kids in Sports

Yogi Berra and Dale Berra

Sandy Alomar and sons Sandy Alomar Jr. and
Roberto Alomar

Bobby and Barry Bonds

Mel and Todd Stottlemyre

Felipe Alou and Moises Alou

Ruben Amaro and Ruben Amaro Jr.

Calvin Hill and Grant Hill

Muhammad Ali and Laila Ali

Joe Frazier and Jacqui Frazier-Lyde

Nate Williams and Natalie Williams

Ken Griffey Sr. and Ken Griffey Jr.

Bobby Hull (known as the "Golden Jet") and
Brett Hull (known as the "Golden Brett")

Jack Nicklaus and Gary Nicklaus

Peter Rose Sr. and Peter Rose Jr.

Bob Duval and David Duval

Lee Petty and Richard Petty

Kyle Rote Sr. and Kyle Rote Jr.

Tony Dorsett and Anthony Dorsett

Cal Ripken and Cal Ripken Jr.

Mario Andretti and Michael Andretti

Dale Earnhardt Sr. and Dale Earnhardt Jr.

What Fathers in History Would Have Said to Their Historical Children

"Put that saber down right this minute!"
Genghis Khan's father

(6)   (6)   (6)

"Didn't I tell you not to chop down that cherry tree?"
George Washington's father

"Don't play with fire!"
Joan of Arc's father

⑤　　⑤　　⑤

"Where did you disappear to?"
Houdini's father

⑤　　⑤　　⑤

"Don't worry. You'll hit your growth spurt."
Napoleon's father

"What's with the knife, Oedipus?"
Oedipus's father

6   6   6

"I told you not to wander too far off."
Columbus's father

6   6   6

"You have to try to get along with the other children."
Attila the Hun's father

"Don't run with those scissors!"
Delilah's father

ⓖ   ⓖ   ⓖ

"So, you got a new girlfriend?"
Henry VIII's father

ⓖ   ⓖ   ⓖ

"That boy sure is bright!"
Edison's father

When Dad's Missing, He's . . .

Piddling around in the yard

ⓖ   ⓖ   ⓖ

Napping on the couch

ⓖ   ⓖ   ⓖ

On the golf course

6   6   6

Underneath the car

6   6   6

In the La-Z-Boy™ on game day

6   6   6

In the workshop

6   6   6

Strategizing for the next big
tee-ball game

6   6   6

Inspecting

6   6   6

Behind the sports page

❦   ❦   ❦

Discussing the virtues of lawn care
with the next-door neighbor

Lessons from Dad

I talk and talk and talk, and I haven't taught people in fifty years what my father taught me by example in one week.

Mario Cuomo, former New York State governor

Dad gave me the confidence to believe in myself. It was the kind of confidence that allowed us to tackle much larger problems, and I think it was a very important factor in my becoming what I am today. . . .

Dr. Joyce Brothers, American psychologist and television personality

ⓖ　　ⓖ　　ⓖ

There was a dynamic that existed in our household that fostered learning, growth, and development. From an early age my dad taught us that we all had purpose and that our purpose was part of a much larger plan. He would often say, "To whom much is given, much is required."

Jesse Jackson Jr., American politician

How true Daddy's words were when he said: "All children must look after their own upbringing." Parents can only give good advice or put them on the right paths, but the final forming of a person's character lies in their own hands.

Anne Frank, diarist

My father taught me how to deal with overly male men: don't react, just say yes and don't pay any attention.

Katharine Hepburn, American actor

Perhaps my willingness to be knocked off a twenty-foot pedestal or shot down a steamship funnel goes back to my earliest happiest days with my father. I *knew* he was going to catch me; I *wasn't* going to get hurt.

Lucille Ball, American actor

⊙   ⊙   ⊙

I just owe everything to my father, [and] it's passionately interesting for me that the things that I learned in a small town, in a very modest home, are just the things that I believe have won the election.

Margaret Thatcher,
former prime minister of England

Papa was, without knowing it, giving us an education in the most real sense. By looking at us, listening to us, hearing us, respecting our opinions, affirming our value, giving us a sense of dignity, he was unquestionably our most influential teacher.

Leo Buscaglia, American educator and writer

His heritage to his children wasn't words or possessions, but an unspoken treasure, the treasure of his example as a man and as a father. More than anything I have, I'm trying to pass that on to my children.

Will Rogers Jr., Native American United States congressman

He taught me the value of a kind word, a hug, catching somebody doing something well and most importantly the helping value of well-earned praise.

Dr. Joy Browne, clinical psychologist and host of radio talk show

I can still look to the example my father set and get the sustenance I need.

Tyne Daly, American actor

[My dad] said that reading about your results was reading about yesterday. As an athlete, you are only as good as today's match. You need to live now to shape your future.

Billie Jean King, American tennis champion

I remember a very important lesson that my father gave me when I was twelve or thirteen. He said, "You know, today I welded a perfect seam and I signed my name to it." And I said, "But, Daddy, no one's going to see it!" And he said, "Yeah, but I know it's there."

Toni Morrison, novelist and essayist

◎　　◎　　◎

My father was brash. He told me: "Don't walk around with your head down." He meant: Don't give up; don't be embarrassed about yourself, stand up and fight.

Shaquille O'Neal, American basketball star

My father was one of my biggest supporters. He always tried to motivate me and, more important, get me to set my goals high. So one day, we just started having a casual conversation. Then in the middle of it, he just said, "You know, you've got to reach for the stars."

Sally Ride, American astronaut and first American woman in space

6   6   6

. . . I do remember one thing my dad told me. After I got fired from one of my first jobs, he said to me, "You're going to have to listen to people that you think you're smarter than."

Chris Rock, American comedian

It's way too hard to understand! I won't be able to write anything that makes sense. . . . My father listened carefully as I listed all of the reasons Nathaniel Hawthorne and I simply weren't going to hit it off. "Martha," he said, "you can do anything. If you put your *mind* to it. *Anything.*"

Martha Stewart,
American lifestyle entrepreneur

My father didn't tell me how to live; he lived, and let me watch him do it.

Clarence Buddinton Kelland,

American pulp writer and screenwriter

But my father influenced more than my political thought. What he is, what he would have hoped to be, has defined me as much as my own dreams. It is a verity of life that *all* fathers cast a long and wide shadow over their children's lives, even if we never meet them. . . .

Ana Veciana-Suarez, columnist and writer

Father's Day Gift Ideas

Robomower (a self-propelling device
that cuts the grass on its own)

🌀   🌀   🌀

Big-screen TV with surround sound

Park Zone PZ-1500 Precise
Parking Device

⟲   ⟲   ⟲

High-powered drill

⟲   ⟲   ⟲

Gift certificate to Monster Racing
Excitement (the company that runs
the driving lessons at Dover Downs)

Sports car with a Global
Positioning System

⟨∅⟩   ⟨∅⟩   ⟨∅⟩

Garmin's Te-Map Garden Water
Computer

⟨∅⟩   ⟨∅⟩   ⟨∅⟩

Titanium driver

A Baron Bob look-alike Comb-Over
Wig (available from Bald is Beautiful
for only $8.95)

⑥   ⑥   ⑥

Subscription to the "Beer of the
Month" club

Things Dads Will Do for You That No One Else Will

Lend you the car keys

⑥   ⑥   ⑥

Twist off a stubborn bottle cap

⑥   ⑥   ⑥

Teach you how to drive

⊚   ⊚   ⊚

Wake you up early and take you out
for a special pancake-and-sausage
breakfast without Mom

⊚   ⊚   ⊚

Not give you a hard time on your
wedding day

Pick you up on the highway when
you've just totaled the family car

6   6   6

Put up the basketball hoop on
the garage

6   6   6

Call for the manager if the soup
is not hot

Let you help with the barbecue

⑥   ⑥   ⑥

Walk the dog in bad weather

⑥   ⑥   ⑥

Volunteer to kill the ugly spider in the
corner of your room

Put together your bike at midnight on
Christmas Eve

⑥   ⑥   ⑥

Buy you coloring books and puzzles
when you're sick

⑥   ⑥   ⑥

Give you his jacket and suffer through
the cold

Pick you up from a bad slumber party

Let you drive while you sit on his lap

Tell you it was a great shot (even if it lost the game)

Animal Fathers

Male seahorses undergo pregnancy and give birth to their sons and daughters.

A father sea catfish keeps the eggs of his young in his mouth until they are ready to hatch. He will not eat until his young are born, which may take several weeks.

A father cockroach eats bird droppings to obtain precious nitrogen, which he carries back to feed his young.

The male Darwin frog hatches his eggs in a pouch in his mouth. When his tadpoles lose their tails and become tiny frogs, they jump out of his mouth.

Although most male ducks live as bachelors, the ruddy duck of North America helps care for his young.

Marmosets are tiny South American monkeys. The fathers take care of their babies from birth: they clean it, then carry it to the mother only when it needs to be nursed. When the baby can eat solid food, the father will feed it.

Rheas are large South American birds similar to ostriches. Father rheas take sole care of their young. From eggs to chicks, they feed, defend, and protect them until they are old enough to survive on their own.

Father emperor penguins protect their eggs, for the over 60-day gestation period, by cradling the egg on their feet and covering it with a feathered flap. Not only do they endure the Antarctic cold for the duration, but they also starve themselves and wind up losing about 25 pounds while they wait for their babies to hatch. Afterward, they feed the chicks a special liquid from their throats.

Since earthworms have both male and female sex organs, every earthworm can be both a mother and a father.

A father Namaqua (sand grouse) of Africa's Kalahari Desert flies as far as 50 miles a day in order to soak himself in water and return to his nest, where his chicks can drink from his feathers.

Male parenting is virtually unknown in insects, but one exception is the giant water bug. The female will latch onto the male until she is ready to lay her eggs, cement as many as 150 eggs onto his back, and then depart.

The male stickleback fish protects not only the fertilized eggs, but also the babies for up to a week after they hatch. After the female lays her eggs, the male fertilizes them and flattens them into a sheet against the bottom of a nest, so that up to seven layers of fertilized eggs may be laid on top. He aerates the eggs by fanning water through the nest, and watches over them constantly, picking out any eggs that die or become moldy.

Paternal care in amphibians is rare, but one exception is the male Panamanian poison-arrow frog. He's responsible for sitting on the eggs and keeping them hydrated with moisture from his skin, and he also bears the job of carrying the newly hatched tadpoles on his back to water.

Father deer mice guard their young when the female goes off to feed. The dads have been observed hovering over the babies, surrounding them with nesting material and even washing them.

Studies of rodent species have shown that pups reared in the company of both parents survive better and grow faster than those reared only by the mother.

Spotted sandpipers are one of a few species of birds that are sex-role reversed; females are aggressive and play the more active role in courtship, while males provide most or all of the care for the young. Males will sit on the eggs for a 21-day incubation period and then tend the babies for another 21 days.

Great Things to Say to Your Dad

"No, I don't need the car; I can just take the bus."

🌀　　🌀　　🌀

"Maybe I should clean my room before I go out tonight."

"Today's homework is all done—now on to tomorrow's."

🌀　　🌀　　🌀

"Why don't I baby-sit the baby while you and Mom go out for a nice dinner?"

🌀　　🌀　　🌀

"I'm sure sex is overrated."

⟲   ⟲   ⟲

"Dad, here's my first paycheck.
Figured I'd give it to you to put toward
my college education."

⟲   ⟲   ⟲

"Party, schmarty—I'd rather stay in and read."

⑥   ⑥   ⑥

"I'm a firm believer in being thrifty."

⑥   ⑥   ⑥

"Long hair, an earring, and a motorcycle? Daddy, he's *so* not my type."

Dad Fashion Trends

Socks with sandals

Hawaiian shirts

Loud ties (usually last year's Father's Day present)

White socks with black shoes

Plaid slacks with print shirts

Wrong-way stripes

Fishing hats (complete with hanging lures)

Brown and navy socks (one on each foot)

Bathrobes with holes in them

Leather jacket (if he's over 40)

Daddy Dearest

No thoughts of fondness e'er appear
More fond, than those I write of here!
No name can e'er on table shine,
My Father! More beloved than thine!
Elizabeth Barrett Browning, English poet

⊙   ⊙   ⊙

Most of us have memories of our fathers, possibly splayed out in front of a Chargers game on TV, in a pair of Hanes irregular that our mother got him. . . .

Stephanie Brush,
author of Men: An Owner's Manual

(6)   (6)   (6)

You know, fathers just have a way of putting everything together.

Erika Cosby, daughter of Bill Cosby

(6)   (6)   (6)

It doesn't matter who my father was; it matters who I remember he was.

Anne Sexton, American poet

You don't have to deserve your mother's love. You have to deserve your father's. He's more particular.

Robert Frost, American poet

Blessed indeed is the man who hears many gentle voices call him father!

Lydia Maria Child,
American writer and abolitionist

⑥　　⑥　　⑥

Directly after God in heaven comes papa.

Wolfgang Amadeus Mozart, Austrian composer

⑥　　⑥　　⑥

There are three stages in a man's life: "My Daddy can whip your Daddy." "Aw, Dad, you don't know anything." "My father used to say. . . ."

Author unknown

It is impossible to please all the world and also one's father.

La Fontaine, French poet

Nowadays a boy cannot follow out a single natural instinct without tumbling over some of those everlasting aphorisms. . . . If he wants to spin his top when he is done with his work, his father quotes, "Procrastination is the thief of time." If he does a virtuous action, he never gets anything for it, because "Virtue is its own reward."

Mark Twain, American writer and humorist

It's only when you grow up, and step back from him, or leave him for your own career and your own home—it's only then that you can measure his greatness and fully appreciate it. Pride reinforces love.

Margaret Truman,
daughter of President Harry S. Truman

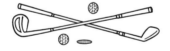

Life doesn't come with
an Instruction Book—that's
why we have a father.

H. Jackson Brown, American writer